ANIMAL MIMICS CONTENTS

WHAT IS MIMICRY?

When creatures pretend to be something they're not, it is called **MIMICRY**. It's much more common than you might think. Insects pretend to be sticks. Caterpillars pretend to be snakes. Spiders pretend to be … poo! What's going on with all this faking?

Mimics often *look* like the animals or things they're copying, but sometimes they also *behave* like them, *sound* like them, or even *smell* like them! **MIMICS**, you see, have **MODELS** – the creature or objects they are pretending to be.

PEPPERMINT STICK INSECT

STAYING ALIVE

Fooling a predator into thinking you're a stick can be a good way to avoid being eaten.

Mimicry is a type of signalling. One creature is the 'sender', and the other is the 'receiver' or target. The bluestriped fangblenny signals that it is a young striped cleaner wrasse so it can pretend to be a cleaner fish and get closer to its prey.

DID YOU KNOW?

We're mimics, too. Babies learn by copying their parents. People also enjoy acting and doing voice impressions.

BLUESTRIPED FANGBLENNY

STRIPED CLEANER WRASSE

STARFISH SHRIMP

Starfish shrimp in the Palaemonidae family live on the underside of a sea star and change colour to mimic the colour of their host.

Most mimics are trying to avoid being eaten, but some are trying to get a meal. Some use their acting skills to attract a mate, and some even try to fool other animals into raising their babies for them!

TRICKY TRAITS

The word mimic comes from the Greek word *mimetikos*, meaning 'imitation'. There are many ways to be a mimic. Mimicry is **DEFENSIVE** when creatures try to fool predators by making themselves look like a leaf, log or stone. Mimics may try to look less dangerous, more dangerous, or sometimes more poisonous than they really are.

A LURKING CROCODILE

FROGFISH

CAMOUFLAGE is sneakily blending in with the environment to go unnoticed. Not all camouflage is mimicry, but if an animal is pretending to be something in particular – such as a floating log or a stone – that's mimicry!

Since predators don't like being caught stalking, putting false eyes on your body may trick them into thinking you're always watching – that's a form of visual mimicry.

AN OWL BUTTERFLY'S BEHIND

Some mimicry is **AGGRESSIVE**. Aggressive mimics may have body parts that look like tasty snacks, luring prey animals in for a look. And then ... CHOMP!

A DEATH ADDER EATING A RAT

TYPES OF MIMICRY

BATESIAN MIMICRY

Many animals use bright colours to say, "Leave me alone! I'm poisonous!" Mimics adopt the colours of deadlier models to send the same message, even if they aren't toxic at all. This is called Batesian mimicry. Harmless king snakes have warning colours similar to deadly coral snakes.

MÜLLERIAN MIMICRY

Poisonous species sometimes mimic similar patterns or warning colours to signal to would-be predators – this is called Müllerian mimicry. Two toxic species that mimic each other are the viceroy butterfly and the wanderer, or monarch, butterfly, which is a species that was introduced to Australia.

MERTENSIAN MIMICRY

Some deadly species may mimic less toxic models to teach predators a lesson. After all, no one learns anything if the predator dies the first time it eats a truly toxic mimic. Deadly South American coral snakes mimic less toxic false coral snakes. This is known as Mertensian mimicry or Emsleyan mimicry.

SCARLET KING SNAKE

EASTERN CORAL SNAKE

VICEROY BUTTERFLY

MONARCH BUTTERFLY

SOUTH AMERICAN CORAL SNAKE

SOUTH AMERICAN FALSE CORAL SNAKE

Can you spot a cryptic mimic hiding here? The Gascoyne pebble-mimic dragon looks like pebbles of mineral quartz. It uses *behavioural* mimicry. If threatened, it curls up and stays as still as a pebble.

VAVILOVIAN MIMICRY

Human agriculture has even led to a type of defensive visual mimicry. When weeds mimic crops to avoid being pulled out or sprayed by farmers, it's called Vavilovian mimicry. For example, rye grass was once just a wild mimic that got confused for wheat, but now rye is considered a crop.

SOME CATERPILLARS MIMIC SNAKES – AND EVEN HISS LIKE THEM!

RYE GRASS

DID YOU KNOW?

Wasmannian mimicry is when one species mimics another (often an ant) to secretly enter its nest or shelter for protection or to steal food.

SENDING SIGNALS

Types of mimicry may be grouped according to the kind of signal being sent. **ACOUSTIC MIMICRY** uses sound. **VISUAL MIMICRY** uses sight. And **MOLECULAR MIMICRY** uses smell!

Some acoustic mimics may be trying to get a meal or to avoid becoming one. For instance, predatory katydids sing just like their cicada prey.

ALBERT'S LYREBIRD

ACOUSTIC MIMICRY is when a creature tries to sound like something else. Some birds use acoustic mimicry to impress their partners. A male Albert's lyrebird can imitate the calls of up to 11 other bird species and can make as many as 37 different sounds!

What's that? Is it a gnarly, broken tree branch covered in rough bark? No. It's a tawny frogmouth!

VISUAL MIMICRY is when a mimic looks like something else by using camouflage or wearing fake warning colours to pretend it is poisonous. Visual mimicry is usually defensive, but it can also be aggressive.

MOLECULAR MIMICRY (or chemical mimicry) is when a mimic smells like something else. It can be used to defend or to attack. Some plants and fungi smell like flowers to attract pollinating insects – others reek of rotting flesh, such as the stinkhorn fungus, to attract flies. European cuckoo wasps mimic the scent of their hosts so they can sneak into their nests.

A tawny frogmouth hunts at night but perches in the open by day, stretching its neck upwards to imitate a tree branch.

HIDING IN PLAIN SIGHT

Camouflaged 'sit-and-wait' predators – such as geckos, or Boyd's forest dragon from Australia's Wet Tropics – stay very still on tree trunks, hiding among the leaves and vines. Under the waves, seahorses, sharks and stonefish use similar tactics, patiently waiting for prey.

HERE BE DRAGONS!

Although less colourful than the chameleons of Africa, many of Australia's dragon lizards have special 'chromatophores' in their skin that help them change colour to blend in with their environment. Other lizards that are experts in disguise are geckos. Leaf-tailed geckos mimic – you guessed it – leaves, or at least their tails do! The rest of a leaf-tailed gecko's body may look like bark, moss, or lichen-covered rocks.

LEAF-TAILED GECKO

BOYD'S FOREST DRAGON

VEILED CHAMELEON

BEARDED DRAGON

Even some eggs are mimics! Most ocean-going sharks give birth to live babies, but Port Jackson sharks live on the ocean floor and lay eggs that look like curly shells or pieces of seaweed. The shape of the eggs helps camouflage them, so they don't get eaten, but also allows them to be wedged into a rocky or weedy seabed to ensure they don't float away.

Stonefish are highly venomous, but they look just like coral or rocks. Can you spot one hiding here?

Tiny 2 cm-long pygmy seahorses match the colours and shapes of the gorgonian corals they cling to and hunt from, making these critters very hard to spot.

PLANT PLAY-ACTING

Praying mantises look like stick insects, but they are fierce **PREDATORS** that use camouflage to hide from the smaller insects they eat. Mantises use aggressive mimicry, whereas stick and leaf insects are herbivores that use defensive mimicry.

The very best plant play-actors are the stick and leaf insects known as phasmids. Even their eggs are mimics and look like plant seeds, tricking seed-eating ants into storing them in the seed larders of the ants' nests!

PRAYING MANTIS

SCORPION STICK INSECT

Insects in the Phylliidae family of South-East Asia and Australia are such good leaf mimics that they're sometimes called 'walking leaves'.

Seadragons are leaf mimics that live in the sea. They drift around pretending to be seaweed and sneakily eating up the tiny crabs and shrimps that try to use them as shelter.

They may look like seaweed, but they're closely related to seahorses, which look like horses but are certainly *not* horse mimics!

COLOURFUL COPYCATS

One of the most common forms of mimicry is dishonest signalling by having fake warning colours. When harmless animals try to look like deadly, poisonous or venomous ones, they're using APOSEMATIC colouring.

When many animals in one place adopt similar warning colours, it can form what is known as a MIMICRY COMPLEX. Australia's many black and golden ant and spider species are such a complex. Many amphibians worldwide are black and yellow, including Australia's endangered corroboree frogs. Aposematic colours are often also good camouflage for species in the wild.

CORROBOREE FROG

YELLOW-BANDED POISON DART FROG

EUROPEAN FIRE SALAMANDER

The harmless harlequin snake eel mimics the colours of the deadly yellow-lipped sea krait.

The common wasp-mimic bee rarely stings, but it adopts the same colours as the much more aggressive potter wasp to trick its enemies.

Many spider species pretend to be ants, including this red-weaver spider from South-East Asia. Unlike the weaver ant that it mimics, it rarely bites.

SPOT THE MIMIC

Animals with warning colouration are often beautiful to look at, but they may be unpleasant or deadly to touch or eat.

In eastern Australia, many nudibranch species (or sea slugs) mimic each other by having similar spots, even if the rest of their colours are totally different. All nudibranchs are poisonous, but some are deadlier than others. In this situation, all members of a mimicry complex win, because their predators quickly learn to leave them all alone!

AN EMPEROR SHRIMP ON A MULTI-PUSTULED MEXICHROMIS NUDIBRANCH

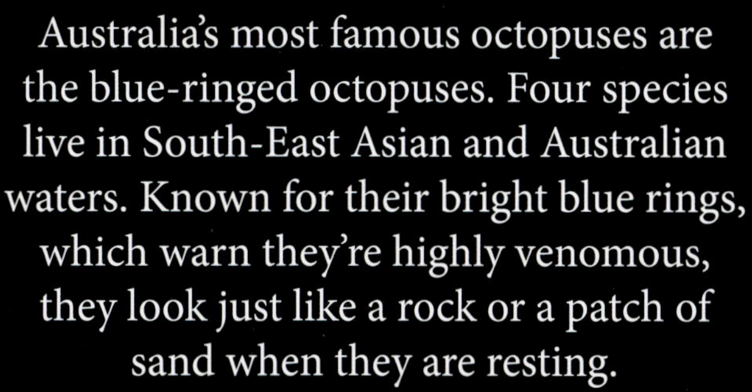

Australia's most famous octopuses are the blue-ringed octopuses. Four species live in South-East Asian and Australian waters. Known for their bright blue rings, which warn they're highly venomous, they look just like a rock or a patch of sand when they are resting.

BLUE-RINGED OCTOPUS

DID YOU KNOW?

The ultimate masters of mimicry are octopuses and cuttlefish. They change both the colour and the texture of their skin to blend in with their surroundings.

The word nudibranch sounds a bit rude, but it just means 'naked gills' because these sea slugs have gills that are outside their bodies, rather than covered up. As their gills are so delicate, nudibranchs use vivid warning colouration to warn other animals to leave them alone.

MARIE'S MEXICHROMIS NUDIBRANCH

SOUTHERN OLD LADY MOTH

EYE SPIES

Using spots to mimic the appearance of a huge, scary face is one of the most common forms of defensive visual mimicry. It's easy to see why. Imagine you're a predator who has spied a butterfly snack. You creep up, ready to pounce, but suddenly … a giant eye! Arrgh! Surely, the eye belongs to an animal much larger than you, so you back off as fast as you can.

MEADOW ARGUS BUTTERFLY

Many butterflies have eyespots on their wings. Some have several, such as the meadow argus. Others have just a couple, such as the southern old lady moth.

You might look at these eyespots and say, "That wouldn't fool me!" Yet the spots only have to startle a predator for a second while the butterfly flies away.

PEACOCK

In America, some caterpillars take eyespot mimicry to the next level. The elephant hawk moth caterpillar not only has eyespots on its behind, but for extra shock factor, it also inflates itself and rears up in a convincing imitation of a snake!

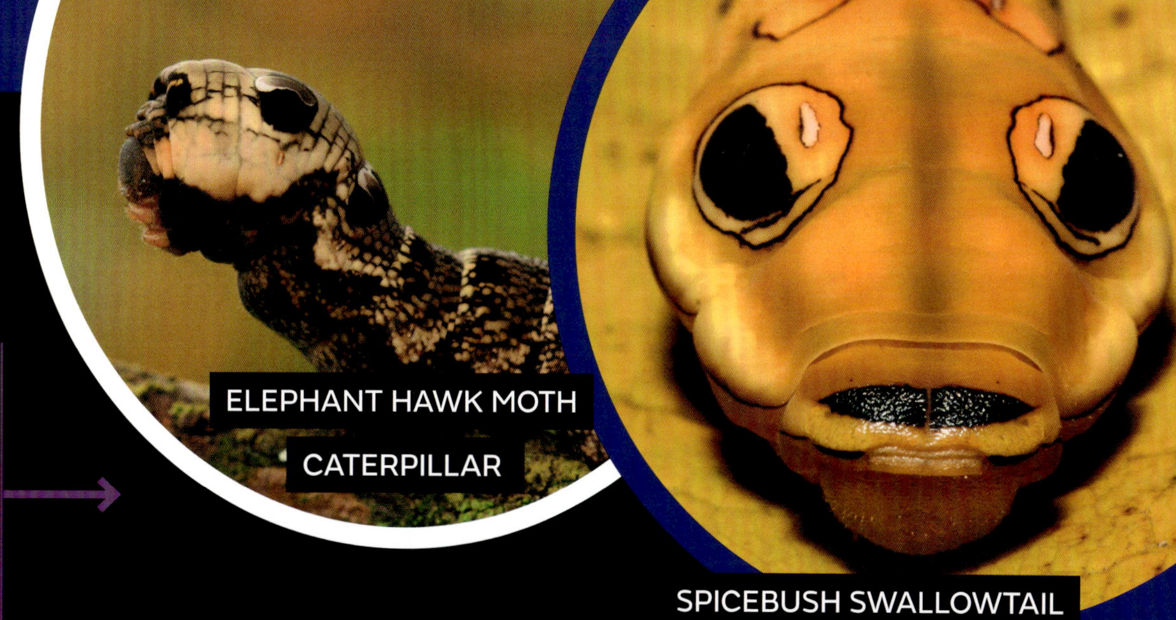

ELEPHANT HAWK MOTH CATERPILLAR

SPICEBUSH SWALLOWTAIL CATERPILLAR

EYE OF THE TIGER

Eyespots are such a great way of confusing lurking big cats that, in some places, people paint eyespots on their cattle's backsides! That may seem strange, yet it seems to work! Eyespots are sometimes used for reasons other than for defensive mimicry. The eyespots behind the ears of some cats, such as the African serval, may encourage kittens to follow their mum on their first adventure outside the den.

The peacock uses eyespots to impress female peahens. Its glorious feathers look like thousands of glittering eyes. Some scientists think this mating display may have evolved from an earlier use of eyespots – defence against tigers.

AFRICAN SERVAL

FIBBING FISH

Eyespots – or **OCELLI**, as they are sometimes known – are very common on fish, too.

If threatened, a comet fish sticks its head in a hole, leaving just its tail – with one large eyespot – in view. A chasing predator may think it is suddenly facing a much bigger fish! The comet's **THREAT DISPLAY** may mimic a territorial white-mouth moray eel poking its head out of its hole.

The truth is that scientists don't always know exactly what eyespots are for. They may just be a pattern that evolved by chance. They might be for defensive mimicry, for camouflage, for use in courtship displays to find mates, or just to help species recognise each other.

LURING LIARS

Not all that wriggles is a worm. It might be the tail of a sneaky snake – the death adder. Some snakes use their worm-like tails as lures to 'fish' for birds or small mammals. This form of aggressive mimicry is called **CAUDAL LURING**, and vipers and death adders excel at it.

A DEATH ADDER USING ITS TAIL AS A LURE

Australia's death adders are masters of motionlessness that use their tails to lure prey in for the kill. If you ever see one, please leave it alone!

HUMPBACK BLACKDEVIL

It's not just snakes (and people) who fish with lures – fish do, too! Anglerfish have lures on top of their heads or dangling in front of their fang-filled jaws to trick curious fish into coming closer … closer … dinner! The tasselled anglerfish does a great impression of a rock covered in seaweed with a couple of tasty worms wriggling on top. Species such as the humpback blackdevil live in the deep oceans, where there's very little light, so their lures also glow. Brilliantly tricky!

POOP STARS

How far would you go to avoid being caught? If your life was on the line, you might go as far as this next bunch of mimics: animals that look like poo! Poop mimicry is more common than you might think – or hope! Let's call these animals 'poop stars'!

Macrocilix maia

WHAT A STINKER!

Perhaps the most spectacularly gross poop mimic of all time is the *Macrocilix maia* moth from Asia, which – incredibly – has a pattern on its wings that looks like two flies eating bird droppings. Ewww!

To make its act more convincing, this moth reeks, too!

The bird-dropping spider is a mimic from southern and eastern Australia. By day, it curls up its legs and pretends to be bird poo. But by night, it becomes more than just a visual mimic! When it gets dark, it uses aggressive mimicry and dangles from a thread of silk, releasing the smell of a female moth to invite male moths to come close enough to be caught – this is a form of molecular mimicry.

The orchard swallowtail caterpillar passes itself off as a big dollop of yucky bird poo.

In South Africa, grass seeds pretend to be poop so that dung beetles will collect them and bury them for regrowth. There's even a poop-mimicking frog from South-East Asia! →

SOUNDS LEGIT

Being a mimic isn't always about looking or smelling like something else. Acoustic mimics try to fool predators or prey by sounding like something else, too. Like visual mimicry, acoustic mimicry can be defensive or aggressive.

MOUSE-EARED BAT

Many bats have amazing hearing and hunt using echolocation, so they can easily identify moths by the sounds they make – unless those moths are mimics!

Mouse-eared bats can be cheeky mimics. To trick owls and avoid being eaten, the greater mouse-eared bat mimics the noise made by European hornets. It's not a hoot for the owls, of course, but it seems like the bats get a buzz out of it!

MAJOR MIMERS

Satin bowerbirds are artists in more ways than one. They make lovely bowers out of sticks and decorate them with bright blue objects they find. They're great dancers. And they mimic the calls of other birds to attract a mate. Bowerbirds mimic crows, cockatoos, and even kookaburras.

SATIN BOWERBIRD

TOXIC, NOT TASTY

Ermine moths live around the world. Like other moths, these deaf moths spend much of their time trying not to get eaten by bats. To avoid being supper, they imitate the sounds of toxic tiger moths. Since both ermine and tiger moths are poisonous or taste awful, this is an example of Müllerian mimicry but also of acoustic **APOSEMATISM**.

LONG-FINNED PILOT WHALES

ERMINE MOTH

DID YOU KNOW?

Acoustic mimicry may be hard to detect because the sounds some animals make aren't meant to be heard by our ears.

Long-finned pilot whales have been heard copying the calls of predatory killer whales in the Great Australian Bight, probably so they can feed safely.

CHICK TRICKS

Birds are the maestros of acoustic mimicry. Some of them copy everything from other bird calls to the sounds of snakes and bees, and even human voices or machinery. They do it for all kinds of reasons – to warn each other of danger, to steal food, to deter predators, or just to impress their mates!

BROWN THORNBILL

If you hear a kookaburra that sounds a little kooky, it may be a lyrebird. Superb lyrebirds can mimic the songs of at least 20 other birds, as well as noises like camera shutters or chainsaws, all while dancing a fancy display that shakes their silvery tail feathers. They're such good tricksters that you might not even notice that 80 per cent of their calls are not their own. They sometimes even copy the copycats and mimic satin bowerbird calls!

Australia's brown thornbill is another clever mimic. It uses its talents to warn other birds of threats. By mimicking the warning calls of various birds, the thornbill acts as a 'security guard' in a flock made up of many different bird species.

LYREBIRDS ARE AMAZING MIMICS

NOT IN MY NEST!

Marsh warblers migrate between Africa and Europe, but they are rare in parts of Europe due to the impact of another form of mimicry – **BROOD PARASITISM**. Brood parasitism is a very aggressive form of mimicry where one animal tricks another animal into raising its babies for it. Super sneaky, right?

CHANNEL-BILLED CUCKOO CHICK AND CURRAWONG

COMMON CUCKOO CHICK (LEFT) AND WAGTAIL

Some insects and fish use this tactic, but the most famous brood parasites are cuckoos, which trick 'hosts' into raising their chicks. Cuckoo eggs often look just like the eggs of their host species. Some cuckoo chicks even mimic the calls of their host's nestlings. Cuckoos don't like sharing, so when a cuckoo chick hatches, it often kills other chicks in the nest. Yes, they are murderous mimics!

The world's largest cuckoo is the channel-billed cuckoo, which lays eggs in the nests of ravens, currawongs and magpies. Its chicks soon outgrow their adoptive parents. Often, an adult pied currawong is totally out-sized by a cuckoo it thinks is its baby.

DID YOU KNOW?

Lyrebirds don't hold the record for stealing songs. European marsh warblers imitate more than 200 other birds, and an African grey parrot has memorised over 1000 words!

CHANNEL-BILLED CUCKOO

TENTACLED TRICKSTERS

Australian waters are home to the world's largest cuttlefish species – the 1 m-long giant cuttlefish. Like other cuttlefish, it can change colour whenever it wants. It can even adopt zebra-like stripes! It uses camouflage to hide from predators or sneak up on prey.

GIANT CUTTLEFISH

DID YOU KNOW?

Humans also mimic other animals. When we copy traits from nature to use in our technology or medicine, it is called **BIOMIMICRY**. Examples include Velcro (inspired by sticky grass seeds or geckos' feet), the wings of a plane (inspired by birds), or submarines (inspired by dolphins).

The flamboyant cuttlefish is known for its flashy mating and warning displays, which don't involve mimicry. But it also spends much of its time pretending to be a stone or an object on the sea floor, complete with rough textures and mottled patterns. This tiny cuttlefish is poisonous, so any predator clever enough to find it might be in for a nasty surprise.

FLAMBOYANT CUTTLEFISH

An octopus can regrow a leg if it loses one. That is one handy (or 'leggy') trait that scientists would love to be able to work out how to copy – maybe one day, we will!

When a mimic octopus copies a venomous animal, that's defensive, but it may also use aggressive mimicry. Pretending to be prey is a clever trap for a predator. This crab-eater pretends to be a crab so it can sneak up on other crabs and eat them. It's like a wolf in sheep's clothing– except it's an octopus in crab's clothing!

A mimic octopus uses both visual and behavioural mimicry to pretend to be all sorts of other creatures, but mostly venomous lionfish, sea snakes and sea jellies. It also spends a lot of time pretending to be a flatfish. No one really knows why. Perhaps it just enjoys acting.

MIMIC OCTOPUS

GLOSSARY

ACOUSTIC MIMICRY
Trying to sound like something else.

AGGRESSIVE
When an animal starts a fight or tries to hurt or kill another animal.

APOSEMATIC
Having warning colours that advertise you're not good to eat.

BIOMIMICRY
When humans 'mimic' designs or traits from nature.

BROOD PARASITISM
Tricking another species into raising your babies.

CAMOUFLAGE
Skin colours or textures that blend in with the surroundings.

CAUDAL LURING
Using the tip of the tail as a moving lure to attract prey.

DEFENSIVE
Something designed to help an animal save its own life.

MIMIC
An animal copying another.

MIMICRY COMPLEX
When many animals have evolved colours or patterns that mimic each other.

MODEL
The animal or thing a mimic is copying.

MOLECULAR MIMICRY
Trying to smell like something else.

OCELLI
Eye-like spots.

PREDATOR
An animal that hunts and eats other animals.

THREAT DISPLAY
A signal to show an animal feels at risk and may attack.

VISUAL MIMICRY
Trying to look like something else.

PICTURE CREDITS

Images are listed clockwise from top left unless specified.
AG = Australian Geographic; SS = Shutterstock.com;
US = Unsplash.com; CP = CanvaPro

Front cover: Cuckoo Marcus Mayer/SS; Somepreaw/SS; CraigRJD/CP; TrapezaStudio/SS; Eric Isselee/SS;Chase D'animulls/SS; Reptiles4all/SS; BarbaraAsh/SS; Kevin Stead/AG; Chase D'animulls/SS; Chameleon'sEye/SS; EdPhillips/SS. **1:** D. Kucharski K. Kucharska/SS; Illuvis/Pixabay; Wright Out There/SS; Richard Whitcombe/SS; Benny Marty/SS. **2:** David Clode/US. **3:** xlchen/SS; orlandin/SS; Johannes Kornelius/SS. 4**:** Sarel/SS; DiveSpin.Com/SS. **5:** Ken Griffiths/SS; Ken Griffiths/SS. **6:** Kawin Jiaranaisakul (Background)/SS; L to R = Radiant Reptilia/SS; Chase D'animulls/SS; Leena Robinson/SS; Christopher O'Donnell/SS; guentermanaus/SS; Ryan M. Bolton/SS. **7:** Kawin Jiaranaisakul (Background)/SS; Brian Bush/Flickr (Top); Aleoks/SS (Bottom). **8:** Geoffrey Moore/US. **9:** Ondrej Prosicky/SS; godi photo/SS; HWall/SS. **10:** L to R = Surapong/SS; Eric Isselee/SS; reptiles4all/SS; David Clode/US. **11:** RugliG/SS; HollyHarry/SS; EdBrown/SS; David Clode/SS. **12:** Lauren Suryanata/SS; DenisDoukhan/Pixabay. **13:** Jacqueline Lee/SS; Pepew Fegley/SS; **14:** Dirk Ercken/SS; Kevin Stead/AG; Rejdan/SS. **15:** Background = Rich Carey/SS; Ethan Daniels; USGS Bee Inventory and Monitoring/Flickr; Frank Prinz; Amrul Fauzi/SS; kajornyot wildlife photography/SS. **16:** Divelvanov/SS. **17:** Background = Kim Briers/SS**;** Richard Whitcombe/SS. **18:** ChameleonsEye/SS; Ken Griffiths/CP; Shawn Hempel/SS. **19:** Miguel Prs/SS; Jay Ondreicka/SS; TrapezaStudio/SS. **20:** Pavaphon Supanantananont/SS; COULANGES/SS. **21:** Bottom = Helmut Corneli/Alamy; Top = Ken Griffiths/SS. **22:** LiCheng Shih/Flickr. **23:** Jansen Chua/SS; Cassandra Madsen/SS (Background); Yutthapong Rassamee/SS; Theuns van der Westhuizen (Etch)/Pexels**. 24:** Agami Photo Agency/SS; Ed Phillips/SS**. 25:** Paco Romero/SS (Bottom left); Imogen Warren/SS; Goldilock Project/SS. **26:** Christian Jude Alexander/SS; CraigRJD/CP. **27:** Svetozar Cenisev/US; Mikhail Vladimirov/SS; David Roy Carson/SS; Markus Mayer/SS. **28:** Illia Kurtin/SS. **29:** Velvetfish/CP; sacit u/SS; Ethan Daniels/SS. **30:** Rosa Jay/SS; Andrew Burgess/SS; sompreaw/SS. **31:** IcyS/SS. **Back cover: SS/Sacit u.**

Australian Geographic

DISCOVER

BOOKS IN THIS SERIES

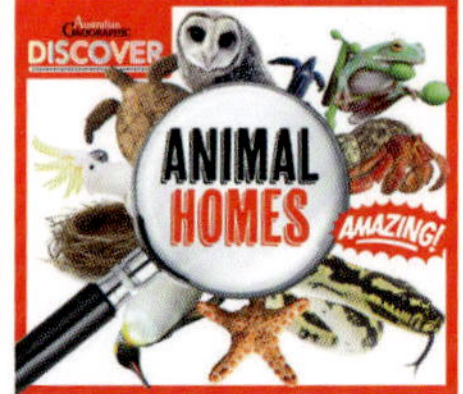

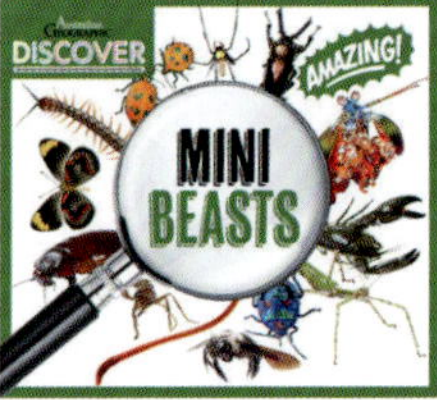

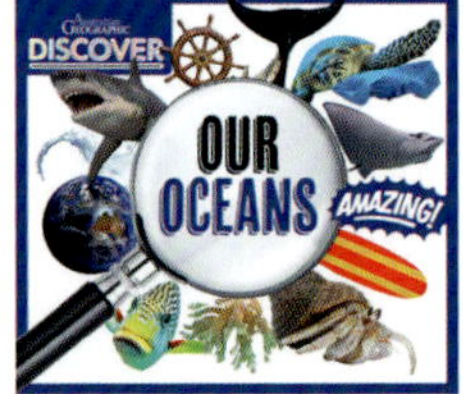

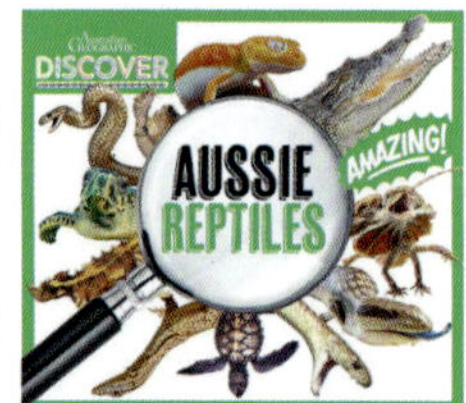

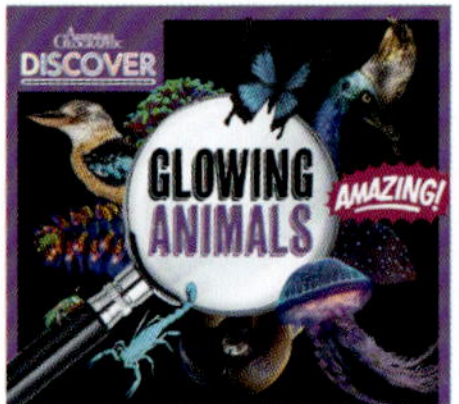

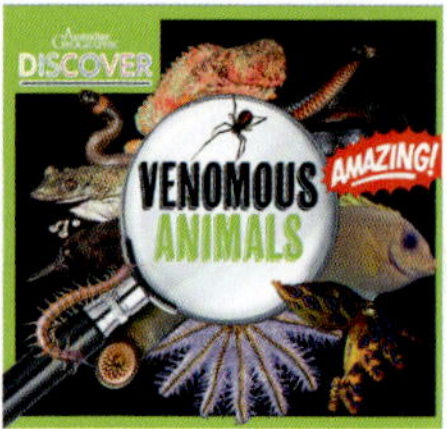

Australian Geographic *Discover: Animal Mimics* is published by Australian Geographic.

First published in 2023
© Australian Geographic Holdings Pty Ltd
52–54 Turner St, Redfern, NSW

editorial@ausgeo.com.au
australiangeographic.com.au

ISBN: 978-1-922388-92-6

Author: Dr Timothy N.W. Jackson
Commissioning Editor: Karin Cox
Creative Director: Aleksandra Beare
Designer: Paul Hodge
Editor: Michele Perry
Print production: Andy Franks

AUSTRALIAN GEOGRAPHIC
Managing Director: David Haslingden
Licensing and Publishing Manager: Tom Bates
Commercial Assistant: Felicity McManus

Printed in China by C & C Offset Printing Co. Ltd.
The paper in this book is FSC® certified. FSC® promotes environmentally responsible, socially beneficial and economically viable management of the world's forests.

Australian Geographic contributes 100% of its profits to the Australian Geographic Society, including its conservation and sustainability programs.